D1544578

DATE DUE

SUPER BIKES

A collection of iconic & much-loved classics

Mason Crest

Contents

Mason Crest
450 Parkway Drive, Suite D
Broomall, PA 19008
www.masoncrest.com

©2016 by Mason Crest, an imprint of National Highlights, Inc.

Printed and bound in the United States of America.

10 9 8 7 6 5 4 3 2 1

Cataloging-in-Publication Data on file with the Library of Congress.

Series ISBN: 978-1-4222-3275-0
Hardback ISBN: 978-1-4222-3282-8
ebook ISBN: 978-1-4222-8520-6

Written by: Mike Hobbs

Images courtesy of Corbis Images, iStock, Moretons and Wiki Commons

Introduction

Welcome to a world that is both vanishing down the end of the straight and yet tantalizingly close at hand. The great thing about superbikes is that they are accessible. By definition, race regulations give you the chance to ride bikes that are very like those sweeping all before them on the track. No one is pretending that they're cheap, of course, but ownership is a strong possibility

– here, super does not mean out of reach.

Rules for the Superbike World Championships demand that the models entering must be similar to those produced and sold to the public, receiving only tuning and

minor adaptations in order to stay eligible. These rules are mirrored for the national championships – the most important take place in the US (the AMA Superbike Championship), the UK, Canada, Australia, and Japan. There are also keenly contested championships in Brazil, China, France, Germany, Holland, Ireland, Italy, New Zealand, South Africa, and Spain.

Therefore, manufacturers must produce (at least) an agreed number of the models for sale so that their superbike can enter these competitions. Generally, profile, appearance, and frame must stay the same, although wheels, brakes, suspension, and swingarm may vary. But for look and feel, your ride can get very close. So, for instance, you, too, like the great Max Biaggi, can ride bikes such as the Aprilia RSV4 1000 or the Factory model, the successor to the Aprilia RSV1000R, on which he became Superbike World Champion in 2010 and 2012 respectively.

This may be the correct technical definition for a superbike since these various championships began, but obviously some models preceded these dates and yet are still worthy of being described as superbikes. Think of the Norton Commando, the Honda CB750, and the Suzuki GT750, which blazed the trail in the late 1960s and early 1970s.

You'll find brief sketches of all these already mentioned here, together with other outstanding models from the four great Japanese marques, including Kawasaki and Yamaha; thrilling American machines, such as those from Buell, Harley-Davidson and MTT; glorious and hugely successful Italian designs from Ducati and MV Agusta; and powerhouse mid-European superbikes from BMW. Many of these bikes have been, at one time, the fastest production bikes in the world. One still is…

They are all, without doubt, superlatively exciting in their different ways. So it's time to begin to follow the magic formula: read, see, ride.

Aprilia RSV1000R

From its base in Noale near Venice in northeast Italy, the Aprilia RSV1000R succeeded the RSV Mille as the stylish company's sport bike in November 2004. As you might expect, this is a lovingly crafted superbike, designed to stand out in a crowd. It can certainly take you places: its fuel capacity is 18 liters (4.6 US gallons) with a 4-liter reserve tank. Bear in mind this is an extremely high-performance race bike which can be a bit tricky to handle on the roads but, if you're experienced, you'll really go to town. Of course it handles like a dream on smooth, well-maintained roads – or on the racetrack. Most reports say it feels more comfortable above the speed limit than below it...

So it's got plenty of low-range torque, is easily muscular enough in mid-range, and has a breathtaking top-end rush. Engine-wise, there's a great angle between the cylinders and the dry sump, which ensures constant lubrication. Noise and traction are both fantastic – everything you'd expect in a superbike. The riding position is especially suitable for tall riders: it is a narrow, exceptionally streamlined design. Pillion accommodation for passengers does not necessarily give them the easiest ride as a consequence.

The higher spec version is the Aprilia RSV1000R Factory. Kitted out in striking gold and black, it offers you sleek extras such as anodized blue forged aluminum wheels, carbon fiber body parts, and fully adjustable Öhlins racing rear monoshock and steering damper. As a result, steering and braking are even smoother on the Factory model than the standard version. Soon after being launched, this model won the Maxisport category for Masterbikes in 2006 as well as taking the overall Masterbike crown for that year. Riders say that the main differences between the two models only really kick in when you start to push the bike as hard as you can.

For those lucky enough to own or ride one, the Aprilia RSV1000R Nera was the de luxe model. Only 200 of these were ever made. It is lighter, with carbon fiber body panels, titanium exhaust, magnesium wheels, titanium nuts, bolts and fasteners, making it weigh around 385lb (175kg), roughly 22lb (10kg) less than the standard model. This enables increased performance from the enhanced V-twin magnesium engine, even though it produces a notch or two less horsepower.

Produced	2004-2010
Engine Size	998cc
Cylinders	2
¼ mile sprint	11 secs
Top Speed	172mph
Power Output	141.13bhp
Transmission	Manual, chain drive
Gears	6 speed
Seat Height	32in (810mm)
Weight	408lb (185kg)
Wheelbase	55.7in (1415mm)

(Specifications refer to the 2004 Aprilia RSV1000R)

BMW S1000RR

Designed and introduced at the BMW Motorrad factory in Munich, Germany in 2008, the BMW S1000RR first raced and came to the market in 2009. There are differences between the production and the racing models but the essential feature is always clear – this superbike is sleek and gives you an exceptionally smooth ride. Reports concentrate on the engine's tractability and flexibility (there is optional electronic traction control)

and the overall delightful feeling of relative weightlessness.

Performance ratings top the charts. In short, it's got unbelievable power and is wonderfully designed – almost too wonderful for some, who comment that this superbike can seem a little soulless. Handling it, however, brings universal cries of joy and the technological advances that BMW have applied, such as the ABS and the traction, are highly rated – you can always turn them

Produced	2009-present
Engine Size	999cc
Cylinders	4
¼ mile sprint	9.57 secs
Top Speed	190mph
Power Output	193bhp
Transmission	Manual
Gears	6 speed, chain drive
Seat Height	32in (820mm)
Weight	183lb (403kg)
Wheelbase	56.4in (1432mm)

(Specifications refer to the 2009 model)

off if that's your preference. The riding position is comfortable, although suspension might suffer on less than pristine tarmac. There can be occasional gear-shifting problems but generally the only other drawback that riders seem to find with it is that it's just too quick and strong for the roads.

A publicity stunt tacitly admitted this. The YouTube video that BMW released in March 2010 to show the S1000RR's acceleration, entitled "the oldest trick in the world," went superviral and amassed 1.4 million views in just 10 days. The trick involved removing a tablecloth from a 20-foot dining table without disturbing the decorations, condiments, and place settings. Even though the trick was later shown to be technically almost impossible, the fact remains that its acceleration is phenomenally fast. The point was made.

In 2010, this superbike was lathered in awards: both *Motorcyclist* and *motorcycle.com* dubbed it Motorcycle of the Year; *Cycle World* named it Best Superbike; *Robb Report* called it the Best of the Best; and the UK's *Motorcycle News* gave it not only Best Superbike over 751cc but also Machine of the Year. During the same year, the Italian rider Ayrton Badovini won every race bar one to sweep all before him in the FIM Superstock 1000 Championship in his native country. The supreme relevance of this feat is that Superstock criteria demand that racing bikes are closest to production models. Given that much of the appeal of superbikes is to ride a version which is like that guided by one of your heroes, it's quite a performance accolade – and an inducement.

Buell 1125R

Produced	2008-2009
Engine Size	1124.9cc
Cylinders	2
¼ mile sprint	10.45 secs
Top Speed	158mph
Power Output	127.1bhp
Transmission	Manual
Gears	6 speed, belt drive
Seat Height	30.5in (775mm)
Weight	466lb (211kg)
Wheelbase	54.1in (1375mm)

(Specifications refer to the 2008 Buell 1125R)

Erik Buell was a former Harley-Davidson engineer who founded his own motorcycle company in East Troy, Wisconsin in 1983. Twenty-five years on he launched the Buell 1125R in 2008, but in October 2009 Harley-Davidson (who had bought a majority stake in 1998) announced that it was discontinuing production of the superbike. Formation of a new company, Erik Buell Racing, meant that the bike and its successors would continue

to compete on the racing circuits.

In its short history the Buell 1125R showed evidence of an admirable tendency to take risks to deliver what the superbike public was looking for: it used a Rotax Helicon powertrain engine from Austria (part-designed by Buell) instead of the Harley-Davidson Sportster middle-weight powertrain and it did not include full fairings, because Buell did not wish to put the bike in the same class as

Japanese sport bikes.

So what's it like to ride a Buell 1125R? Well, it's obviously powerful, without giving you the impression that the power is seemingly limitless, as can be the case with some superbikes. Even so, there is a tendency for the front wheel to reach for the sky when you slam on the power, so you have to stay alert for that. A steering damper might have been a useful addition but, in general, handling is said to be pretty manageable. And the good thing is that the power kicks in relatively early, making it ideal for that special road buzz. In terms of design, you pay your money and you take your choice – for instance, some love the idiosyncratic radiator cowlings and some are not so keen (although they might prove very helpful in a spill). But there's no doubt the relatively short-lived model was full of individuality.

With a strange irony, two championships were won on the Buell 1125R models – straddling either side of the announcement that the factory was ceasing production of all but racing versions. In September 2009, Danny Eslick won the AMA Pro Racing Championship, securing the title at New Jersey Motorsports Park. Then, in November 2009, Hector Arana made sure of the NHRA Pro Stock World Championship at the Southern California NHRA finals. By that time, the Buell 1125RR was going into race-only production with some changes including a titanium exhaust, magnesium wheels, full fairings, and a chain drive.

Ducati 916

The Ducati 916 has been generally acknowledged to be the most beautifully designed bike of the last 30 years. Massimo Tamburini, the designer, came up with a revolutionary new model after intensive work at the company's shared research base in San Marino, the tiny principality nestling within Italy. Style and technology, performance and symmetry, all came together to produce an immaculate machine – one outstanding enough to win many world championships as a racer but also to feature prominently in the 1998 Guggenheim Exhibition on The Art of the Motorcycle.

Produced	1994-1998
Engine Size	916cc
Cylinders	2
¼ mile sprint	10.9 secs
Top Speed	159.7mph
Power Output	114bhp
Transmission	Manual
Gears	6 speed, chain drive
Seat Height	31in (790mm)
Weight	429lb (194.5kg)
Wheelbase	56in (1410mm)

(Specifications refer to the 1994 model)

14

So what was it that made the Ducati 916 such a technological advance? First, it was much smaller than its predecessors, yet sleek and powerful. It featured a stylish sharp nose, a single-sided swing arm, patented adjustable steering, an exhaust system with twin mufflers exiting just underneath the seat, and one of the most distinctive styling jobs ever seen on two wheels. And it scooped up all the Motorcycle of the Year awards going because it was unique in its beauty and charisma. It truly changed the face of sports bikes.

All this, however, would have been rendered redundant if the bike had not delivered where it counts – on the road and on the track. The Ducati 916 handled like a dream, and set new standards for braking and all-round performance. The significantly revised 916cc V-twin engine developed by Massimo Bordi gave it a more even torque spread (at the cost of slightly less power). Even today, riders still purr over its performance, although some say it is not the most reliable or comfortable of bikes. But, the bike's many happy owners still swear by the model years later. The crucial thing is that it makes them smile, and only a really worthwhile icon does that.

This superbike, as you'd expect, was an immensely successful racer. Carl Fogarty won the Superbikes World Championship in 1994, 1995, and 1998, while Troy Corser won the title in 1996. Moreover, Fogarty went on to be World Champion in 1999 on the bike's successor, the Ducati 996, as did Troy Bayliss in 2001 – and Ducati claimed the Constructors' Championship from 1994-2001 (with the exception of 1997). So, when you ease yourself into the saddle, you know you're riding a real world-beater!

Ducati 1098

Ducati made a bold bid in 2007 to reestablish their dominance over the superbike world with the 1098, which also came in two other models: the 1098R and the 1098S. The 1098 shared more design elements with the older 998 model than with its immediate predecessor the 999, such as horizontally placed headlights and a non-integrated exhaust system. Another carryover from its iconic 916/998 heritage was the single-sided swingarm. This return to a more traditional Ducati design was warmly welcomed by many fans, who had criticized the design of the 999.

The proof of the pudding was in the eating. Riders found that performance was incredible: the 1098 offered the highest torque-to-weight ratio of any production sport bike ever made. With its terrific Testastretta Evoluzione engine, acceleration was similarly fantastic as a result. Even today, handling is exquisite. The forks combined with the standard Pirelli tires allow you to explore the far side of leaning and

make you revise what you thought was possible on a motorcycle. They also give amazing feedback – combine that with a really neutral chassis and you've got probably the best handling 1000-class road motorcycle ever. Enthusiasts say you can be clumsy with it, hang-off or not hang-off, and the Ducati 1098 will do exactly what you tell it, letting you bounce from curb to curb.

The bike was garlanded with awards. *Moto*, *Australian Motorcycle News*, and *Motorrad* all made it Bike of the Year for 2007. The Motorcycle Design Association awarded it Best Design and Best Sportsbike. It was named International Motorbike of the Year for both 2007 and 2008 by a combination of the world's motorcycle journalists and moto-communities. It also received numerous Best in Show awards at gatherings both in Italy and abroad.

With the release of the 1098, Ducati created a stir not only with road riders, but also in the racing world, specifically the Superbike World Championship. Ducati won the 2008 Superbike World Championship with Troy Bayliss in his final season before retirement, along with the 2008 British Superbike Championship through Shane "Shakey" Byrne, and then also won the 2011 Superbike World Championship through Carlos Checa with its 1098R. After 2011, Ducati retired from formal participation in the Superbikes

Produced	2007-2009
Engine Size	1099cc
Cylinders	2
¼ mile sprint	10.55 secs
Top Speed	180mph
Power Output	160bhp
Transmission	Manual
Gears	6 speed, chain drive
Seat Height	32.3in (820mm)
Weight	381lb (173kg)
Wheelbase	56.3in (1430mm)

(Specifications refer to the 2007 version)

Championships, instead making models available for privateer teams. As a tribute to Bayliss, the company produced about 500 bikes in particular colors and specifications – the Ducati 1098R Bayliss Limited Edition.

Ducati 1198

From the company based in Bologna, Italy, the Ducati 1198/1198S is a sport bike made from 2009 to 2011. For the 2011 model year there were two versions: the 1198 and 1198SP (which replaced the 1198S). The 1198 naturally shared some design elements with its predecessor, the 1098, but it has more power and torque, redesigned wheels, lighter headlights, traction control, and lighter fairings (on the S model), together with a few minor paint changes. One leftover from its distant 998 heritage is the distinctive single-sided swingarm.

Reports are uniformly favorable. Nobody else has a 168bhp V-twin on its books, complete with traction control, Öhlins suspension, and data-recording, and, if they did, it wouldn't have the same devastating performance all wrapped up in a chassis that has more character than Gina Lollobrigida. Riders can rest assured that this engine is one serious powerhouse. Torque alone gets the Ducati 1198S shifting the earth backward on its axis, and then the power takes over to make point-to-point roads seem like a model racetrack. Happily, the gearbox is sweeter than a nut, and

the lump doesn't vibrate anywhere near as badly as you think a mighty V-twin should.

Since the original 1098, all the models in Ducati's superbike

Produced	2009-2011
Engine Size	1198cc
Cylinders	2
¼ mile sprint	9.75 secs
Top Speed	185mph
Power Output	168bhp
Transmission	Manual
Gears	6 speed, chain drive, dry multi-plate clutch
Seat Height	32.3in (820mm)
Weight	373 b (169kg)
Wheelbase	56.3in (1430mm)

(Specifications refer to the 2009 Ducati 1198S)

range now feel more similar to Japanese output to ride – there's plenty of room behind the bars, with standard seat-to-bar-to-peg dimensions. This bike is designed for fast-flowing corners and consequently struggles to stay on line in the tightest of tight corners, but as the ride height and suspension are fully adjustable it just needs time and care to get the ride geared toward the rider.

Several years of V-twin production should mean Ducati has those reliability issues that affected earlier models sorted out. Obviously the bike has a serious amount of electronic aids, but even so electrics are not a big issue with Ducati since they've done a major revamp of their working methods over recent years. If you want, you can get Öhlins road and track forks and rear shock, a traction control system that is eight-way level adjustable, with a facility to record, download, and replay throttle position, speed, gear, and traction control activity. Riders claim there's a lot to be said for the race-spec Brembo front brakes and it would be all positive. There may no longer be works models in the World Championships – but you can still ride them.

Ducati 1199 Panigale

At the time of its release, the Ducati 1199 Panigale was the world's most powerful production twin-cylinder engine. Without doubt, the 1199 has the highest power-to-weight and torque-to-weight ratios among production motorcycles. Whereas previous Ducatis had belt-driven overhead cams, this engine's valvetrain uses gears and chain. The engine serves as a stressed member, enabling the Panigale to be smaller and lighter than a conventionally framed motorcycle. The 1199 is also one of the first production sports motorcycles to feature electronically adjustable suspension. Rebound and compression damping is adjusted electronically while pre-load is

Produced	2011-present
Engine Size	1198cc
Cylinders	2
¼ mile sprint	9.9 secs (2012 model)
Top Speed	186mph
Power Output	195bhp
Transmission	Manual
Gears	6 speed, chain drive, multi plate clutch
Height	32.5in (825mm)
Weight	362lb (164kg)
Wheelbase	56.6in (1437mm)

(Specifications refer to the 2011 model unless otherwise stated)

still adjusted manually. The 1199's exhaust system and mufflers are underneath the engine, not beneath the seat as on previous models.

Ducati seems to have done it again: this is a mold-breaking motorcycle. Apart from the color and the noise it makes, the Panigale has nothing in common with Ducati superbikes of old. The chassis is frameless, there's a new-generation superquadro engine, and it comes with the very latest electronic rider aids, which actually work. This bike, riders say, has a smooth power curve and a searing top end. Like Ducatis of old it's extremely stable round fast corners, but now it steers as fast as a Japanese superbike. It's a very clever motorcycle and very, very good.

The Panigale is devilishly fast but controllable; the throttle response is smooth, and the power delivery linear. The 1198's excess of lowdown torque has been tempered, which makes the 1199 more controllable under hard acceleration. It has a new gearbox, a wet slipper clutch, and a ride-by-wire throttle system for the first time. The riding position is completely different to former Ducati superbikes and there's a far shorter stretch to the bars than before, which keeps you more in control. It's incredibly light and has the kind of Fireblade-like stability the 1198 could only dream about.

With the S model's electronic riding modes, you can alter the electronic suspension's settings, power, throttle response, engine braking, and traction control on the move. This lets you have the Panigale smooth, docile, and comfortable on motorways, or sharp, responsive, and fiery on your favorite road or track.

Forget the old myth that Ducatis are unreliable, because they just aren't anymore. Modern-day Ducatis are as dependable as Japanese bikes and don't cost a fortune to service. A purple 1199 Panigale featured in the movie *Kick-Ass 2*, ridden by Hit-Girl. Go on – outride her.

Harley-Davidson VRSC models

Produced	2002-present
Engine Size	1131cc
Cylinders	2
¼ mile sprint	11.5 secs
Top Speed	130mph
Power Output	115bhp
Transmission	Manual
Gears	5 speed, belt drive
Seat Height	44.9in (660mm)
Weight	606lb (275kg)
Wheelbase	67.2in (1710mm)

(Specifications refer to the 2002 Harley-Davidson VRSCA V-Rod)

In 2001, the Harley-Davidson VRSC (it stands for V-Twin Racing Street Custom) modern family of cruiser motorcycles was introduced in a single model called the V-Rod. It was billed as the year Harley goes high-tech after decades of merely updating their lovable antiques. In 2002, the Harley-Davidson VRSCA V-Rod was the first of the VRSC Rod family to come to market. It was developed by Harley-Davidson to compete against Japanese and American muscle bikes and made use of the Revolution engine, developed jointly with Porsche that, for the first time in Harley production history, featured overhead cams and liquid cooling.

The V-Rod is visually distinct from other Harley-Davidson motorcycles. It can be easily identified by the 60-degree V-twin engine, the radiator, and the hydro-formed frame members that support the round-topped air cleaner cover. Another distinct difference between the V-Rod and all other Harley production motorcycles is the location of the fuel tank underneath the seat,

placing the rider on top of it rather than the usual frontal placement. The "tank" in this case is simple dressing, hiding the frame. Loosely based on the VR-1000 superbike, it continues to be a platform around which Harley-Davidson builds drag-racing competition machines. All VRSC models are produced at Harley-Davidson's Vehicle and Powertrain Operations facility in Kansas City, Missouri.

There were plenty of technological innovations. The Harley-Davidson VRSCA V-Rod's water-cooling, loads of power, with handling that could embarrass a badly ridden sports bike and brakes that stop fast, were totally novel on a Harley. A great deal of time went in to designing this superbike and there are no serious glitches in terms of reliability. The finish on the bike is better than the air-cooled Harleys but if you do let it corrode, it'll not do the second-hand value any favors at all – but most Harley-Davidson VRSCA V-Rods are

sunny weekend toys not winter sluggers anyway.

Riders say the superbike gives more power than a Ducati 916 or early Honda Fireblade and is far smoother than Harleys of old. The injected V-twin engine is just chuggy enough but pleasingly torquey at low revs. But as the needle sweeps into the top third of the tacho, the exhaust note changes and it lays down some serious power. Tuned Harley-Davidson VRSCA V-Rods are competitive on the drag strip – and the long, low styling echoes that. There are few frills on the standard model and it carries a small fuel tank. The riding position's not like any other bike: the seat's low, as are the bars, and the pegs are extremely far forward. It's not a comfortable position for most people but at least you can dip into the enormous range of accessories. The modern tires and modern suspension allied to a modern chassis give up-to-date handling. It is great on left-hand

bends, say some, but take a right hander at any pace and the exhaust decks out disappointingly soon. It's a real shame, although the brakes are very capable and the suspension manages to balance sport and comfort nicely.

Of course, some diehards refuse to accept them but the Harley-Davidson VRSCA V-Rod remains a tempting package. It began its production life in 2002 and ceased in 2006 and has since been succeeded by a host of models: the VRSCB V-Rod (2004-05), VRSCSE Screamin' Eagle CVO V-Rod (2005), VRSCD Night-Rod (2006-08), VRSCSE2 Screamin' Eagle CVO V-Rod (2006), VRSCSR Street-Rod (2006-07), VRSCDX Night-Rod Special (2007-present), VRSCX V-Rod (2007), VRXSE Destroyer (2007), VRSCAW V-Rod (2007-10), and finally, the VRSCF V-Rod Muscle (2009-present). Chances are you'll find a model that suits you among one of these family members.

Honda CB750

This is the daddy of them all. Honda introduced the CB750 motorcycle to the US and European markets in 1969 after experiencing success with their smaller motorcycles. The bike was targeted directly at the US market after their officials, including founder Soichiro Honda, repeatedly met with US dealers and reported

Produced	1969-2003, 2007
Engine Size	747cc
Cylinders	4
¼ mile sprint	12.4 secs
Top Speed	128mph
Power Output	73bhp
Transmission	Manual
Gears	5 speed
Seat Height	31in (790mm)
Weight	473lb (215kg)
Wheelbase	57.3in (1460mm)

(Specifications refer to the 1992 F2 model)

the opportunity for a larger bike. Under development for a year, the CB750 offered two unprecedented features: a front disc brake and a transverse straight-four engine with an overhead camshaft, neither of which was previously available on a mainstream, affordable production bike. The CB750 was the first modern four-cylinder machine from a mainstream manufacturer, and the term superbike was coined to describe it. The bike offered other

important features that added to its value: electric starter, kill switch, dual mirrors, flashing turn signals, easily maintained valves, and overall smoothness and freedom from vibration both underway and at a standstill; later models (from 1991 on when the F2 version was developed) included maintenance-free hydraulic valves.

In contrast, 1992's Honda CB750 F2 may not have been the most exciting motorcycle to leave the Honda factory but it was a competent, comfortable cruising motorcycle nonetheless. Adequate suspension, good riding position, top brakes, and a strong engine are its plus points but the F2 is let down by average handling and a lack of real zest. Sadly, according to some riders, it can feel rather boring. The engine is taken from the Honda CBX750 and detuned – it's a smooth, powerful engine with a lot of torque and enough top end to keep most people happy. With the motorcycle best treated as a cruiser, its strong but laidback

acceleration means it's hardly hair-raising stuff, but that's rather the point. As you would expect, the delivery's super-smooth. The Honda CB750 F2 is equipped with clear but basic clocks, apt for the retro look, but they're plastic-like and look a bit cheap. There's no fuel gauge either, so you'll have to remember it does 41 miles per gallon, with a range of 181 miles. On the upside, there's loads of room for both riders and pillions: comfort's a strong point. The mirrors work well and the CBR600-derived brakes are excellent. There are some handy touches including a grabrail and a centerstand.

The Honda CB750 F2 has a tallish, upright seating position, with wide bars and a good turning circle, which sound good for town work, but the motorcycle is heavy and this can let it down. Motorways and highways are where the bike is most at home, while fast, twisty lanes show up its lack of focused handling. The gears can also be a bit clunky. Still, well built and

finished, it is certainly a trustworthy friend. It should also last: plenty of the original 1970s Honda CB750 models are still going. The suspension isn't bad but on older motorcycles it'll definitely need some sprucing up: engine-wise, you're looking at a long-distance runner that is also pretty simple to maintain.

The model of the original superbike is included in the AMA Motorcycle Hall of Fame Classic Bikes, featured in the Discovery Channel's Greatest Motorbikes Ever, and sits in the UK National Motor Museum. It was also in The Art of the Motorcycle Exhibition at the Guggenheim. In 2007, Honda announced the sale of a new CB750 very similar to the models sold in the 1970s. The company promoted two models: the CB750 Special Edition in the silver colors of the CB750 AMA racer of the 1970s, and the CB750, offered in three color schemes reminiscent of CB750s sold previously.

Honda CBR1000RR Fireblade

Known in many countries as the Fireblade, the CBR1000RR is a 998cc liquid-cooled inline four-cylinder sport bike introduced by Honda in 2004 as the seventh generation of the series of motorcycles that began with the CBR900RR in 1992. Since 2004, there have been several versions of the Fireblade, each of which has many admirers: the eighth-generation RR model appeared in 2006, followed by further models for 2008, 2009, 2010, and 2012. Every new model brings in significant upgrades and tweaks to tempt would-be owners.

So what's the original 2004 model like to ride? It's cold, calm, and supremely effective – an exceptional sports bike that's blisteringly fast on the road or track, according to reports. It is bristling with MotoGP technology and, compared to previous Hondas, the bike can seem manic and much faster but also heavier and, paradoxically, less exciting too. Fairly standard for its class, the 998cc in-line four-cylinder engine may not make headlines but has to be tried to be believed – seamless, effortless power thrusts the motorcycle to incredibly high speeds. Chances are, say riders, you'll run out of bottle before the Fireblade runs out of shove. Honda's (then) best fuel injection is reasonably smooth.

Mass centralization helps it handle in a neutral, stable way. Standard suspension settings are too hard for most road bikers but it's fully adjustable so you can tweak it to suit your own style. The Fireblade is dripping with comparatively innovative technology in what can be a conservative class that thrives on small power increases and weight losses. Rotary steering damper on the model can be altered electronically on the hoof, and clocks are very comprehensive – although it's a shame the underseat storage has been sacrificed due to the exhaust location. The riding position is quite racy. Generally excellent reliability is reported and build quality is above average. Some motorcycles use a massive amount of oil – the company says that the model only has a problem if consumption exceeds a liter every 800 miles – so it's best to keep an eye on the level.

For comparison, reports on the 2009 model focused not on its new, oval-shaped indicators, but its revolutionary electronically

Produced	2004-present
Engine Size	998cc
Cylinders	4
¼ mile sprint	10.6 secs
Top Speed	178mph
Power Output	172bhp
Transmission	Manual
Gears	6 speed, close-ratio
Seat Height	32.3in (820mm)
Weight	396lb (180kg)
Wheelbase	55.6in (1410mm)

(Specifications refer to the 2004 CBR1000RR)

controlled combined ABS system, making it the world's first ever ABS-equipped superbike. This system takes none of the enjoyment out of riding the superbike – it feels just the same to ride as a normal Blade, even on the track.

Riders claim the system stays in the background until the moment you get into a difficult braking situation, then the brake-by-wire kicks in. This is a landmark motorcycle and surely the shape of things to come. It might not have the ultimate power of its rivals, but the magic of the Fireblade is its grunt and searing acceleration. Impressively, it can do 150mph in a quarter of a mile. The power is easy to use, all

the way through the rev-range, and the throttle response is perfect. This is one of the all-time great engines. The suspension is plush and soaks up bumps on the road nicely, while giving lots of support and control on the circuit.

The CBR1000RR was awarded *Cycle World*'s International Bike of the Year for 2008-09 by the world's moto-journal communities and journalists. This model captured

the Best Sportbike of the Year award in *Motorcycle USA* Best of 2009 awards, having also won the over 750cc open sportbike class in 2008. The 2012 CBR1000RR won another *Cycle World* shootout, as well as *Motorcycle USA* Best Street and Track comparisons. James Toseland (UK) won the second of his Superbike World Championships on an adapted Fireblade in 2007.

Honda CBR1100XX

Produced	1996-2007
Engine Size	1137cc
Cylinders	4
¼ mile sprint	10.3 secs
Top Speed	178.5mph
Power Output	164bhp
Transmission	Manual
Gears	6 speed, close-ratio
Seat Height	32in (810mm)
Weight	492lb (223kg)
Wheelbase	59in (1490mm)

(Specifications refer to the 1997 model)

You won't be in much doubt for very long. The Super Blackbird is a useable, comfortable, tidy handling sports tourer but also a ballistic powerhouse. This Honda machine is paradoxically both sensible and utterly insane at the same time – in one nicely presented package. In short, say enthusiasts, it's one of the best all-round motorcycles out there. The rivals to its crown are plentiful but none match this proven motorcycle.

The Super Blackbird's in-line four-cylinder engine is a conventional layout but it works well, producing acceptable low-down power, muscular mid-range, and a top-end rush that gobbles up any straight in seconds. Twin balance shafts mean it's so smooth it can be rigid mounted, making the superbike both lighter and stiffer overall. It's extremely reliable, a major advantage: problems with the machine are almost non-existent even at huge mileages. It is admirably neutral

Also known as the Super Blackbird, the Honda CBR1100XX was produced between 1996 and 2007. This superbike was developed to challenge the Kawasaki Ninja ZX-11 as the world's fastest production motorcycle, and Honda duly succeeded in capturing the title – which it held until 1999 – with a top speed of 178.5mph (287.3km/h). The Blackbird is named after the Lockheed SR-71, also a speed record holder.

Production of the Super Blackbird began in 1996 (sales from 1997) and halted in 2007. Imports to North America ended in 2003 but sales continued in Europe until 2007. Major changes were introduced in 1999, when Honda switched from carburetors to PGM fuel injection. The 2001 Blackbird received an LCD instrument cluster. Since then, it's been mostly color changes, with alterations to the exhaust and fuelling systems to meet emission standards and maintain or improve fuel efficiency.

What's it like to ride the bike that used to hold the record as the fastest production motorcycle?

and stable – but there's no getting away from the fact that it's heavy, since it weighs 492lb. The latest sports bikes come in under 380lb so on tight roads, if you're riding in a pack, you may get left behind a little. Front and rear brakes are linked – it's an effective system that works well in the wet but experts may dislike it and overhauls are costly.

There's absolutely no doubt the Super Blackbird was a range topper in its day, meaning it's reasonably well spec'd up. Comfort's pretty good, although the bars have to be quite low due to the high top speed. Some owners boost low-speed comfort with bar risers, lifting them about an inch. Many also add a double bubble screen as well for increased wind protection. As befits Honda, the build quality is better than pretty much anything out there on two wheels. Some Super Blackbirds get pressed into service as long-distance, year-round commuters and show few signs except tatty fork leg lowers. Very occasionally, cam chain tensioners and regulator rectifiers can fail – like almost every Honda four.

In the February 1997 issue of *Sport Rider* magazine, the CBR1100XX was tested at a top speed of 178.5mph, compared with 175mph for the ZX-11. Its supremacy over the ZX-11 was confirmed in April 1997 by *Motorcycle Consumer News*, although the speeds achieved were slightly lower and the margin was therefore narrower. Having achieved its aim, the Super Blackbird held sway until in 1999 the Suzuki Hayabusa GSX1300R overtook it as the world's fastest production bike with a top speed of 194mph – although the dizzyingly escalating top speeds resulted in a gentleman's agreement to limit these to 186mph to stave off possible import bans.

Honda CBX1000

Produced	1978-1982
Engine Size	1047cc
Cylinders	6
¼ mile sprint	11.36 secs
Top Speed	118mph
Power Output	105bhp
Transmission	Manual
Gears	5 speed
Seat Height	32in (810mm)
Weight	600lb (272kg)
Wheelbase	58.9in (1495mm)

(Specifications refer to the 1979 version)

Now here's another venerable old master from the Japanese production line in Minato, Tokyo. In the late 1970s, the four major Japanese motorcycle manufacturers all began the process of building superbikes: road bikes with superior performance. Honda intended the CBX to help re-establish the company's position at the forefront of motorcycle technology. For its time, the engine was highly advanced, Honda having started the move toward four valves per cylinder.

At the time, there was a growing sense that Honda had become conservative. The company's marque street bike, the four-cylinder Honda CB750, had been hailed as a wonderbike during the late 1960s but was growing old. Honda's other offerings were reliable, dependable, and well-engineered, but then again, so are most fittings. The Honda

CBX was introduced in 1978 as the first production motorcycle with an inline six-cylinder engine (earlier they had produced an RC series six-cylinder race bike). Since other models in the series were launched, the CBX is often referred to as the CBX1000.

Honda set out to firebomb its rivals. It assigned the design work to a new, competition-trained generation of engineers headed by 37-year-old Shoichiro Irimajiri, who had created Honda's 250cc and 297cc six-cylinder GP race engines. The engine, developed in about 18 months, remains a masterpiece.

Spanning 23.4in, it's only 2in wider than the power plant of the CB750. The 33-degree forward angle of the cylinders, combined with a V-shaped manifold that angles all six carbs toward the centerline of the bike, maximizes legroom. And while bike technology has blown by the CBX over the years, the old flagship still gets attention. There had never been anything quite like the CBX when it was introduced in 1978. Some bikes attract good reviews – this one got praise somewhere above heavenly. *Cycle Guide* praised the bike as "the Vincent Black Shadow of

1979" upon its introduction.

In 1981, Honda switched tack and headed the bike into the sport touring category with the CBX-B, adding a sleek fairing and panniers, as well as Pro-Link single-shock rear suspension and air-adjustable front forks. Dual stainless-alloy ventilated front rotors (a first for the motorcycle industry) were added to offset its weight. When the 1982 CBX-C model arrived, it was nearly identical – the only differences being paint and trim. But although it lasted less than five years, its style gave birth both to Honda's sport bikes and to its ST series.

Kawasaki GPZ900R

Produced	1984-1996 (US) -2003 (Japan)
Engine Size	908cc
Cylinders	4
¼ mile sprint	10.97 secs
Top Speed	151mph
Power Output	113bhp
Transmission	Manual
Gears	6 speed, chain drive
Seat Height	31in (780mm)
Weight	503lb (228kg)
Wheelbase	58.9in (1495mm)

(Specifications refer to the 1984 Kawasaki GPZ900R)

The 1984 GPZ900R was the first Kawasaki bike to be officially marketed (in North America) under the Ninja brand name.

In spite of its great power, the GPZ900R was smooth and easy to ride in urban traffic, owing to the new suspension and a crankshaft counter-balancer that almost eliminated secondary vibration. The fairing's aerodynamics combined with good overall ergonomics to make comfortable long-distance riding possible.

In 1984, the new Ninja was the cutting-edge of performance, with

Welcome to another one of the great Old Masters. The Kawasaki GPZ900R (also known as the ZX900A or Ninja 900) was manufactured from 1984 to 2003, the earliest member of the Kawasaki Ninja family of sport bikes. The 1984 GPZ900R (or ZX900A-1) was a revolutionary design that set the blueprint for the modern-day sport bike. Featured in the movie *Top Gun*, starring Tom Cruise, it became a cultural icon.

Technical advances included water cooling and 16 valves, allowing additional power, and a frame that used the engine as a stressed member for improved handling and reduced weight –as a result of testing that showed the standard downtubes carried virtually no weight and could be eliminated. Its top speed gave it the title of the fastest production bike at the time, with standing quarter mile times of 10.976 seconds – or 10.55 seconds recorded by specialist rider Jay "Pee Wee" Gleason.

an all-new liquid-cooled four-cylinder engine driving its cams from the left side instead of the middle – the better to lean over farther in corners and produce top-end power that put the big air-cooled multis of the day to shame. Thirty years later, the old beast reminds us why Kawasakis used to be thought of as unbreakable but a bit crude: on one model, black primer shows through the red paint on part of the fairing and many of the stickers are just that, stuck on. None of it mattered; in 1984, the target rider was nearing 30 years old, doing well, and cruising the boulevards after work in Oakley Blades with slicked back long hair.

Never mind the period hyperbole, your open-class streetbike of 1984 was also a pretty good daily ride/sport-tourer. The old Ninja weighed 546 pounds with half a tank of fuel (2.9 gallons). But don't let the look of the bike put you off. This was something very special at the time and it still gives a good account of itself today. That motor might have been fast, but it was easy to use and flexible too. It is very smooth even in heavy town traffic, although prolonged urban riding needs the hydraulic clutch to be in perfect nick and you'll see the temperature gauge working overtime before the fan cuts in (many owners fit a manual fan switch to cool the engine at their discretion).

At the core of that ease of use is the counter-balancer on the crankshaft, which keeps vibration down. By modern standards the GPZ revs slowly and the real power doesn't come in till late, but back then it was a missile. Yet it wasn't just the engine, or the chassis. This was Japan's first fully faired sports bike and that fairing works very well, allied to an upright riding position which means you can do some serious miles on the Kawasaki.

Take the bike into the curves and it comes alive. The eager engine is easy to punch out of corners and there are no surprises from the stable and competent chassis, providing, of course, that the 26-year-old suspension is still working properly and you remember that cross-ply tires don't ride the same as radials...

Kawasaki ZX-10R Ninja

The follow-up to the ZX-9R, the Kawasaki Ninja ZX-10R/ ZX 1000 E was originally released in 2004 – with minor revisions added in 2005. Compact, with a short wheelbase and a high power-to-weight ratio, which helped the handling, it combines an ultra-narrow chassis, low weight, and radial brakes. Kawasaki engineers utilized a stack design for a liquid-cooled, 998cc inline four-cylinder engine. The crank axis, input shaft, and output shaft of the engine are positioned in a triangular layout to reduce length, while the high-speed generator is placed behind the cylinder bank to reduce engine width. The exhaust system was fully titanium with a single muffler.

In 2004 and 2005 the ZX-10R won Best Superbike from *Cycle World* magazine and the prestigious international

Produced	2004-present
Engine Size	998cc
Cylinders	4
¼ mile sprint	10.7 secs
Top Speed	180mph
Power Output	181bhp
Transmission	Manual
Gears	6 speed
Seat Height	32.5in (825mm)
Weight	386lb (175kg)
Wheelbase	54.7in (1390mm)
(Specifications refer to the 2004 model)	

Masterbike competition. It billed itself as the ultimate track bike – one of Kawasaki's first machines after the firm gave itself a shot in the arm in 2002. One wild ride, it's a formidable weapon in experienced hands. It's light, generates massive power, and handles superbly on the track – a bit of a handful on the road, though. The 181bhp is never going to be anything other than a rush. It can't quite match the GSX-R for low-down drive but get the revs up, say riders, and it's hard to fault.

It's civilized and flexible enough at lower revs to make pottering a possibility, too – although that's not really what the bike's for.

Effortless and precise, it's as easy to chuck about as a 600 and pretty stable regardless of whether you're easing through town or hurling it around on a race or track day. Brakes are incredibly strong too. Like all modern sports bikes it can be twitchy and isn't for the inexperienced.

Styling is minimal but not without a few extras. There's a shift light which you can set to remind you when to change gear. The instrument cluster can appear unclear to some – the LCD rev counter sweeps round the edge and isn't as obvious as an old-fashioned needle gauge. The big four Japanese marques all produce pretty solid

bikes these days and Kawasaki is no longer a league behind its rivals. That said, fasteners, brake hose connections, wheels, brackets, and brake calipers can suffer if used in winter. No major reliability problems have shown up yet.

Among other changes, the 2006 model featured twin underseat exhausts which contributed to an increase in dry weight. The engine remained largely unchanged. The 2006 model carried over to 2007, with only color scheme changes. But it was all new for 2008: there was a dramatic change in appearance with the bike featuring a much more angular front end. Kawasaki moved away from twin-underseat exhausts to a more conventional single side exhaust. The compression ratio of the engine was raised. Slight changes for 2009 included upgraded Öhlins steering damper and transmission, and revised bodywork.

The 2011 ZX-10R underwent a major overhaul mechanically and visually. Notably, Kawasaki introduced their S-KTRC (Sport Kawasaki Traction Control) system as a standard feature, responsible for predicting when traction will be lost and adapting accordingly. Also new were KIBS (Kawasaki Intelligent Braking System) as their optional ABS system, a design overhaul, adjustable foot-pegs, larger throttle bodies, a horizontal rear suspension, lighter three-spoke wheels, Showa Big Piston Fork (BPF) front suspension, and an LCD panel dashboard. The 2012 model was identical to 2011 with slightly different paint schemes offered. In 2013 the models had another small revision where the colors changed again and an Öhlins electronic front steering dampener was added – plus a boost when Tom Sykes (UK) won an exciting Superbike World Championship.

KTM 1190 RC8

The KTM 1190 RC8 is a revelatory sport bike: the first generation 2008 model had a 1148cc V-twin engine and was the Austrian manufacturer's first-ever superbike design. The RC8 model was supplemented with RC8R models one year later in 2009 – the RC8 designation had its last year of production in 2010. Current models from 2009 through 2013 use a 1195cc V-twin engine, with a Twin-Spark design debuting on the 2011 model.

It's unashamedly a circuit-based blaster, say experts, that will need a rider to be fully aware of what he is about to buy if it's to be used on the road. This bike cries out for corners to be taken at speed, although it doesn't need to be ridden hard to appreciate it. But when it is given its head the rewards are stupendous. For enthusiasts it's styled to be different, made to please. New models have the same LC8 engine as used on the current crop of large capacity KTM machines but

with capacity increased to 1195cc and additional tuning work (new cams and timing, compression hike, and so on). It's a gutsy lump down below and matched with an impressive amount of top-end drive. The driving force is the linear torque output that makes riding the KTM RC8R as easy as opening the throttle.

There were some gearbox problems on the RC8, but the RC8R is an upgrade, thanks to a new gear selector mechanism and

Produced	2008-present
Engine Size	1195cc
Cylinders	2
¼ mile sprint	10.77 secs
Top Speed	169mph
Power Output	159bhp
Transmission	Manual
Gears	6 speed
Seat Height	31.7in (805mm)
Weight	401lb (182kg)
Wheelbase	56.1in (1425mm)

(Specifications refer to the 2009 RC8R model)

revised gear cluster cogs. It comes with road or track throttle tubes: the road version has a chamfered cam to smooth out low rpm throttle delivery. Increased trail figure makes it a more stable bike through long sweepers but still allows quick steering nimbleness through the twists. Front and rear suspension is race quality and has suitable adjustment (high and low speed compression adjustment at the rear) to dial in the bike to suit anyone and all road/track conditions – settings are found under the seat.

WP suspension as a product doesn't have the brand name and desirability of Öhlins when really, say enthusiasts, it should have – the suspension on the RC8R is apparently belting. Marchesini-forged wheels are par for the course on a grade-A superbike as are the Brembo Monobloc race-spec brakes. But other areas will tickle your fancy: adjustable footrests, levers, handlebars, subframe position, and rear ride height are all there and easy to achieve.

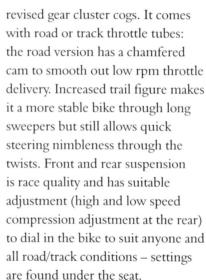

MTT Turbine Superbike

The Marine Turbine Technologies (MTT) Turbine Superbike, also known as the Y2K Turbine Superbike due to its 2000 launch, is a wheel-driven motorcycle powered by a turboshaft engine. When MTT president Ted McIntyre decided to add a motorcycle to his firm's range, he appointed Christian Travert, a former bike racer and custom builder, to head the project.

The machine is powered by a Rolls-Royce-Allison Model 250 gas turbine producing 320shp at 6000. Unlike some earlier jet-powered motorcycles, where a massive jet engine provided thrust, the turboshaft engine on this model drives the rear wheel via a two-speed gearbox and chain and sprocket. The engines used in the superbikes are second-hand, having reached the FAA-mandated running time limit, after which they have to be rebuilt, regardless of condition. To get around the problem of procuring the kerosene usually used in turbine engines, the engine is also able to use diesel or jet fuel.

In 2008, MTT promised to launch a more powerful Streetfighter version, another turbine bike with a proposed 420shp from the Allison 250-20b engine, but it was never released – the original bike only featured the standard 320shp shaft turbine. Due to the converted three-speed

Produced	2000-2005
Engine Size	250 c18 turboshaft
Cylinders	12
¼ mile sprint	9.8 secs
Top Speed	200 mph
Power Output	320shp
Transmission	Semi-automatic
Gears	2 speed
Seat Height	33.1in (840mm)
Weight	500lb (230kg)
Wheelbase	68in (1727mm)

(Specifications refer to the 2000 model)

gearbox and right-angle bevel drive, the power loss was quite high and the bike only made around 270shp at the rear wheel. It has never achieved a speed close to the advertised 250mph: many people feel it is impossible because it does not generate enough horsepower.

It's still breathtaking. *Greatest Ever Motorcycles*, a Discovery Channel television show, ranked the Turbine Superbike the fourth greatest motorcycle, stating that it held a Guinness World Record for the world's fastest production motorcycle, and that it was also the most expensive. Jay Leno, who had owned a Turbine Superbike for almost four years at the time of the broadcast, said: "It really does scare you half to death, but it's great fun." Needless to say, other owners are thin on the ground. The acceleration is a bit mental, according to one rider – if you can hold on to the handlebars the superbike will reach 227mph from a standing start in 15 seconds. However, in the same show, the bike was claimed to have "as much relevance to motorcycling as a fish" – even Leno introduced it as "really a stupid motorcycle." If you want a controversial superbike, you've found it.

MV Agusta F4 1000

Coming from MV Agusta's famous base near Milan, the new F4 1000 product line began with a special edition called the F4 AGO in 2005. The bike came with special graphics displaying the number 1 in a yellow oval, referring to MV Agusta's racing heritage and superstar rider Giacomo Agostini. Only 300 bikes were produced. The first mass-produced model, the F4 1000S, was released in 2005 and came with a 166bhp engine. Riders were promised 0-60 in 2.7 seconds and a top speed estimated at 190mph. You could add a pillion for a brave passenger.

The F4 Tamburini is a special edition of the F4 1000 S, also released in 2005. It was the first F4 to be equipped with the Torque Shift System, which varies the length of the intake trumpets with speed in order to provide optimum torque at low and high engine speeds. Engine output was a claimed 128 kilowatts (172bhp) and alleged top speed was 190.6mph. All the bodywork was carbon fiber

except the fuel tank. Again, only 300 were produced. The bike is named after its legendary designer Massimo Tamburini, who had joined from Ducati.

Enthusiastic riders claim the 1000S blends a monster engine, God-given handling, and heart-aching beauty to be one of the most desirable two-wheeled creations of all time. The fuelling isn't perfect at the bottom end, with a fluffy response that needs to be balanced with more gas and a heavy clutch around town. On the open road nothing short of a six-figure supercar or a jet fighter even comes close. With the Marzocchi forks and Sachs shock (fully adjustable of course – the shock comes with high- and low-speed compression damping for added finessing) the F4 tracks as true a line as any train. It will lean for Italy, says one rider, with only your courage and ability the true limiting factors. The six-piston Nissin brakes aren't radial, but they're brilliant. Should your pockets be deep enough there are

race exhausts, MV leathers, carbon fiber bodywork, and covers available from the factory. An Öhlins steering damper is standard.

The superbike's componentry is top drawer, but the build standards remain somewhat suspect, despite new quality controls brought in by Proton. Wise owners say keep it well away from salty roads and preferably rain, too. Fair enough – for the world's fastest production motorcycle (312, since 2007).

Produced	2005-present
Engine Size	998cc
Cylinders	4
¼ mile sprint	11.4 secs
Top Speed	190mph
Power Output	166bhp
Transmission	Manual
Gears	6 speed
Seat Height	31.9in (810mm)
Weight	412.3lb (192kg)
Wheelbase	79.02in (2007mm)

(Specifications refer to the 2006 F4 1000S)

Norton Commando

So we come to the granddaddy of them all. The Norton Commando is a British Norton-Villiers motorcycle with an OHV pre-unit parallel-twin engine, launched in 1967. Initially a nominal 750cc displacement, in 1973 it became an 850cc model. The revolutionary part of the Commando, compared to earlier Norton models, was the award-winning frame developed by former Rolls-Royce engineer Dr Stefan Bauer. The first production machines completed in April 1968

Produced	1967-1975, 2010-present
Engine Size	750cc
Cylinders	2
¼ mile sprint	12.69 secs (1969)
Top Speed	115mph
Power Output	58bhp
Transmission	Manual
Gears	4 speed, chain
Seat Height	33-34in (838.2-863.6mm)
Weight	420lb (190kg)
Wheelbase	56.75in (1441mm)

(Specifications refer to the 1967 Commando unless otherwise stated)

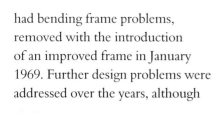

had bending frame problems, removed with the introduction of an improved frame in January 1969. Further design problems were addressed over the years, although some persisted to the end.

The original model, the Fastback, was joined by the scrambler-style S Type which had a high-level left-side exhaust and a 2.5-gallon tank. The first Commandos had a twin-leading-shoe front drum brake. The production racer, featuring a tuned engine, front disc brake, and finished in bright yellow, was known as the "Yellow Peril." In March to June 1970 the updated S, the Roadster, featured the 750cc engine, low-level exhaust, and upward-angled silencers with reverse cones. September 1970 saw the introduction of the classic Fastback Mk2, which had alloy levers with modified stands and chain guards. The Street Scrambler and the Hi Rider were launched in May 1971, and the Fastback Long Range, with increased petrol tank capacity, from July 1971. The Combat engine was introduced in January 1972, which also saw the appearance of the Mk4 Fastback, updated "Roadster," and the "750 Interstate."

Originally, says one owner, it broke down a lot with little things mainly (points, valve guides, and such) and it took a year or two to learn what to do with it, but since then it has been fine. However, the age of the machines means it can be difficult to find one. But there can be re-launches…

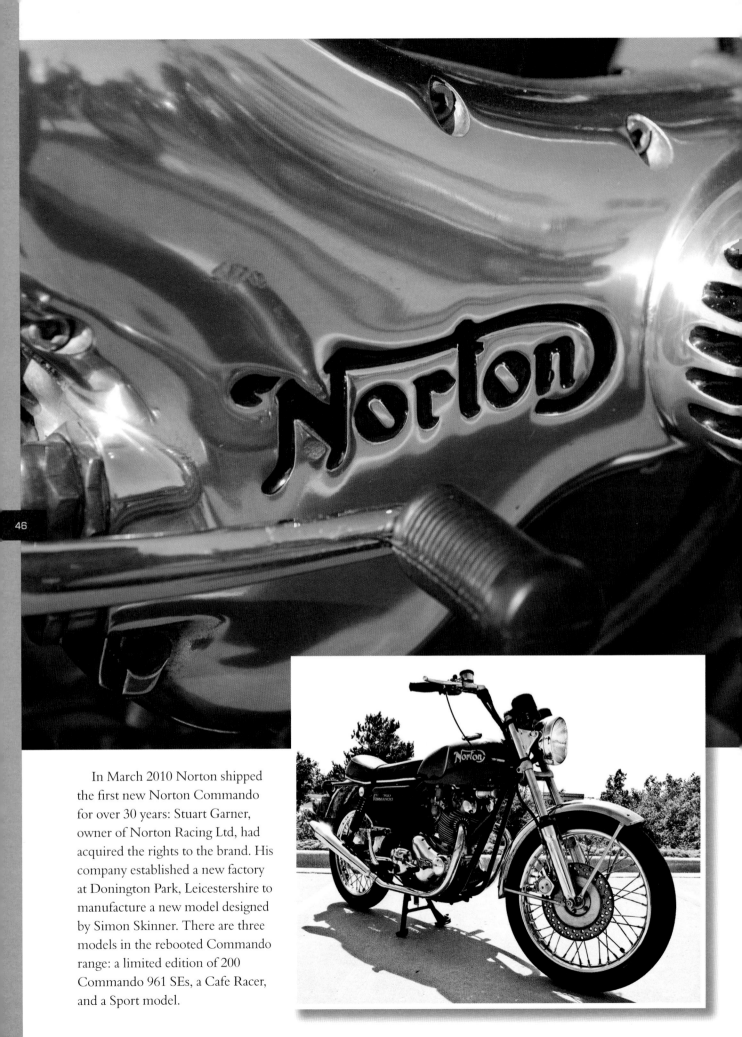

In March 2010 Norton shipped the first new Norton Commando for over 30 years: Stuart Garner, owner of Norton Racing Ltd, had acquired the rights to the brand. His company established a new factory at Donington Park, Leicestershire to manufacture a new model designed by Simon Skinner. There are three models in the rebooted Commando range: a limited edition of 200 Commando 961 SEs, a Cafe Racer, and a Sport model.

How are these to ride? According to reports, the revived Norton's new Commando 961 SE is a great feel-good bike. It gives riding and owning pleasure by the skip-load and is a machine you'll park up and spend hours admiring in the garage.

There were bound to be a few teething troubles, most notably a flat spot around 5000rpm. Even so there's much to praise. It has plenty of low-down grunt from around 2000rpm, snicks through its gears happily enough, and makes an addictive growl. Horsepower feels about right and is enough to give riders a kick. The chassis is simply ideal: it's neutral feeling yet with enough sporting prowess to have fun. Light, slim, and sharp steering, it is flickable, with, of course, incontrovertibly good suspension and brakes. Adjustment is available if needed.

As a straightforward, old-style roadster, it is fairly basic in terms of equipment – there's obviously no luggage, fairing, and added extras. But what it has is top-notch: wheels, switchgear, and instruments are all among the best there is, as befitting a Special Edition model. It's hand-built, using some of the best components available anywhere in the world so quality, on face value at least, is top drawer.

Suzuki GSX-R750

This Suzuki GSX-R750 – the "Gixxer" (as it's known) – is a 750cc class sport bike from the marque's GSX-R series of motorcycles. It was introduced in 1985 and can be considered one of the first of the modern racer-replicas with many race-derived technologies and the looks of a Suzuki Endurance racer at an affordable price.

How do recent models ride? After years of gentle evolution Suzuki went to town on its 2011 GSX-R750, according to reports. Weighing in at 418lb fully fuelled and ready to go, it's a massive 17lb lighter than the old model, giving the 148bhp a mouth-watering power-to-weight ratio. The 750's rolling chassis and bodywork was completely new, but it didn't get the GSX-R600's radical engine overhaul and the resulting 2lb extra weight reduction. Aside from minor revisions to make it breathe more easily, the 750's motor was essentially the same as before, but it now spins up faster and makes greater low- and mid-range power. It still has the perfect mix of power and handling, but thanks to the lighter weight, acceleration is now more toward the expected level of a superbike. It feels longer-legged in the higher gears on track, but it does make for a less frantic machine on the road.

It's fun, fast, and handles beautifully, but crucially it's very easy to ride at high speeds, unlike a bigger sports bike. There are only minor changes to the 148bhp, 750cc inline-four-cylinder motor. It now has pentagonal-shaped (instead of round) ventilation holes in the block, which apparently reduces pumping losses inside the engine and creates more bottom-end power. The primary injector nozzles are changed from 41 to 35 degrees inside the throttle bodies.

Produced	1985-present
Engine Size	750cc
Cylinders	4
¼ mile sprint	10.45 secs
Top Speed	175mph
Power Output	148bhp
Transmission	Manual
Gears	6 speed
Seat Height	31.9in (810mm)
Weight	418lb (190kg)
Wheelbase	54.7in (1389mm)
(Specifications refer to the 2011 model)	

The gearbox remains the same. A revised, more efficient ECU has been moved from under the seat to the top of the airbox to save weight on the length of wiring loom. Blip the throttle, say riders, and you still get that angry, metallic rasp from the airbox and exhaust. The revs spin up almost as quickly on the move, racing through the gears, as at a standstill. The GSX-R750's performance is as much as you'll ever need on the road or track.

It's still civilized, comfortable and, thanks to adjustable foot-pegs, roomy enough for tall riders too. The suspension is plush on the move and there's lots of adjustment for track riding. Showa big piston forks give lots of support and feel, while Brembo Monobloc calipers are a big improvement: they still tend to fade on track, but not as much as before. With much less weight to lug around, the bike is a joy to ride fast. It loads you with feedback and flatters your riding. There are few bikes that can cover ground as fast and are such fun at the same time. The new chassis has a shorter wheelbase, so steering is even lighter than before. In the real world, the GSX-R750 is every bit as fast as a 1000.

Compared to the latest 1000s, it is sparsely equipped, but that's the way it's supposed to be: it's light, simple, and fast. It does have a speed-sensitive, electronic steering damper and two power maps, which are easily switchable from the left bar. There's a new dash, which incorporates a gear position indicator and lap timer. In terms of reliability, GSX-Rs will never let you down. They'll take any abuse you throw at them all day long – they seem to actually enjoy it. Build quality is very good, but the paint finish isn't as deep as some machines and can stone chip easily.

Suzuki GSX-R1000

Introduced in 2001, the Suzuki GSX-R1000 is another sport bike from their "Gixxer" series of motorcycles. Powered by a liquid-cooled 999cc inline four-cylinder, four-stroke engine, it was built to replace the GSX-R1100. It was not just an enlarged version of the GSX-R750, although it shared many features with its little brother. The main frame is the same in both models, but the material used on the big brother was 0.020in (0.5mm) thicker. Suzuki claimed the torsional rigidity of the frame had increased 10% in comparison with the GSX-R750.

This 2001 Suzuki GSX-R1000 is the real deal – the top dog sports bike of its day. Later versions became smaller and more revvy as well as even faster round circuits

Produced	2001-present
Engine Size	999cc
Cylinders	4
¼ mile sprint	10.6 secs
Top Speed	180mph
Power Output	160bhp
Transmission	Manual
Gears	6 speed, constant mesh
Seat Height	32.7in (830mm)
Weight	374lb (170kg)
Wheelbase	56in (1410mm)
(Specifications refer to the 2001 model)	

and, arguably, easier to handle. The original K1 and K2 models are still supremely competent sports bikes and pretty decent all-round machines. It has always had the strongest engine in the 1000cc sport class – that makes it king of the gods.

The bike, riders claim, has huge power on tap just above tickover, a walloping mid-range and a top-end rush to give you goosebumps. Lower ratios means earlier versions can outperform later models in top gear. It's pleasantly raw with enough gruff edge to excite as well. It is capable of leading the fast group at track days or winning races but useable and stable on the road. Steering is not super fast but it's still a nimble bike.

Really hard use can show up weaknesses in the front brakes. Try fresh fluid and pads but if they don't work, a Brembo 1920 master cylinder should help. Amazingly for a class-leading (and maybe even class-redefining) hardcore sports bike, it's pretty comfortable too. A sensible riding position (maybe the pegs are a bit high for all-day riding) plus soft gel-filled seats and a decent fairing mean you can tour contentedly. There's some underseat storage and reasonable mirrors and headlights, too. The finish is generally pretty robust: the gold-colored Titanium Nitride coating flakes off the front forks but it's only a cosmetic problem. Gearbox problems are not unknown if the bike is ridden very hard – which probably means track use. The odd engine problem occurs but owners say they're easy to work on for a big, potentially complex engine. And in 2005, Troy Corser won Suzuki's first ever Superbike World Championship on an adapted model.

Suzuki GT750

Here's another venerable master: the GT750 was made by Suzuki from 1971 to 1977 and was the first Japanese motorcycle with a liquid-cooled engine. This bike had a water-cooled, two-stroke, three-cylinder engine that provided good acceleration over a wide speed range. Technologies developed for Grand Prix racing were incorporated into the body structure and brakes. Easily visible meters and other features were also provided. The motor was essentially an existing twin design with an extra cylinder. With a large (later chromed) radiator, the cooling system made for more weight, but it did help to increase the engine's longevity. It had a five-speed gearbox and three-into-four exhaust.

The prototype Suzuki GT750 was shown at the 17th Tokyo Motor Show in October 1970 and launched in September 1971 as a sports tourer (GT standing for Grand Turismo). Marketed as the Le Mans in the US and Canada, it was nicknamed the "Water Buffalo" in the United States and the "Kettle" in Britain. Its smooth yet strong delivery was a hit with riders. Style married content: the Society of Automotive Engineers of Japan includes the 1971 Suzuki GT750 as one of their 240 Landmarks of Japanese Automotive Technology.

In 1973 the updated model was announced with extra chrome plating and two 11.61in discs replacing the drum front brake. No other manufacturer was offering dual front disc brakes at this time, so this was quite a marketing coup for Suzuki.

What are these old groundbreakers like to ride? In standard guise with their large radiator and massive chrome exhaust system they attract a lot of attention and admiration. Though a little soft in the ride, they are extremely comfortable and capable touring machines. With its 68bhp it's not going to worry many people but it does require a firm grip when riding through twisty minor roads. According to riders, you get a full appreciation of this torque-filled engine as you accelerate. It's a fantastic feeling and rewards you with that great engine howl…

Most owners prefer to keep their bikes in standard trim and will go to extraordinary lengths to maintain them as Suzuki built them. From 1971 to 1977 these bikes rolled off the production line and out to riders – they're still loved some 40 years later. There remains a cult following throughout the world for the Suzuki GT750 and all members are devoted to this trailblazing motorcycle.

Produced	1971-1977
Engine Size	739cc
Cylinders	3
¼ mile sprint	13.87 secs
Top Speed	110mph
Power Output	68bhp
Transmission	Manual
Gears	5 speed, chain final drive
Height	44.3in (1130mm)
Weight	482lb (219kg)
Wheelbase	57.5in (1460mm)

(Specifications refer to the 1971 model)

Suzuki Hayabusa/ GSX1300R

Produced	1999-present
Engine Size	1299cc
Cylinders	4
¼ mile sprint	10.4 secs
Top Speed	190mph
Power Output	160bhp
Transmission	Manual
Gears	6 speed, constant mesh, chain drive
Seat Height	31.7in (805mm)
Weight	474lb (215kg)
Wheelbase	55.5in (1485mm)
(Specifications refer to the 1999 model)	

Made since 1999, the Suzuki Hayabusa (or GSX1300R) is a sport bike that immediately won acclaim as the world's fastest production motorcycle (until 2000, when Kawasaki snatched it back), with a top speed of 188 to 194mph. Devotees dub the original Hayabusa still one seriously quick motorcycle, possessed of enormous acceleration and breathtaking top speed. It's true, it doesn't quite handle all that power (and weight) too brilliantly sometimes, but it remains a supremely comfortably long-range missile that always delivers a shot of raw adrenaline. And those in the know say the latest version's better yet.

The original GSX1300R is a very simple, yet brutally effective, four-cylinder beast. Its 1299cc engine is bulletproof, doesn't chin fuel too badly at semi-sane speeds, and the fuel injection works very efficiently too. The amount of mid-range torque that the Hayabusa produces is especially impressive and makes fast road riding ridiculously easy. The new version is even quicker though, according to some reports. However, the machine does have some handling issues. First off, it has a semi-touring kind of ride, with softish suspension that allows the front end to squirm and move around under hard braking. And talking of brakes, the Hayabusa's tend to fade a bit under repeated hard use from 150mph plus speeds – which, since you're asking, are achieved in about 12 seconds.

Enthusiasts say that as a sports-tourer it's definitely more touring than sporty in its overall handling. That ugly fairing works very well, not only at punching holes in the atmosphere at 180mph, but at keeping bad weather off the rider too – some riders say the new version's better still. Good headlight coverage, comfortable rider and pillion accommodation, four bungee hooks, and some

underseat storage – plus throwover panniers can be made to fit – combine to make the superbike a more than capable tourer. It has an excellent grabrail, too.

Reliability is generally excellent, although some owners say that rear wheel bearings have been known to collapse occasionally at relatively low miles. The real problem with long-term Hayabusa ownership is the quality of the finish on many components, which is poor. It rusts, it pits, it discolors its alloy, unless you really keep on top of it and clean every nook and cranny. Exhausts have been known to rot, too. But that speed…

Yamaha VMAX

The mighty Yamaha V-Max, called the VMAX since 2008, is a cruiser motorcycle known for its powerful V4 engine, shaft drive, and distinctive styling. Basically the VMAX is what happens when you mix 1679cc and nearly 200 horsepower in a motorcycle that's part cruiser, part sport bike. Riders gasp that it's difficult to explain just how quickly it builds speed. Cruise along at 30mph in second gear, pick up the throttle and hold on tight... you'll be doing 90mph before you realize. So it's a thrill ride of epic proportions – the VMAX redefines the word torque – the kind of acceleration that you feel in your chest. The type you don't soon forget – and it handles well into the bargain.

The VMAX's engine produces a claimed 200bhp (or 197.4bhp) at just 9000rpm. To put that into perspective, that's the same as a GP replica Ducati Desmosedici RR, but at 4000rpm less. To achieve this, the new model borrows heavily from latest sports bike technology, meaning that – looks aside – it has little in common with its predecessor. Crucial new features are the adjustable intake funnels, fly-by-wire electronic throttle, a high compression ratio, and forged aluminum pistons.

It works, too – you can expect the kind of bulletproof quality and reliability that has become standard on all new Japanese motorcycles. The main frame is an all-new, cast aluminum diamond with a die-cast and extruded rear subframe. There are some quality parts dished out as standard, including a hi-tech info-center on the tank and Brembo brakes with wavy discs. What's more, the VMAX's signature aluminum intake covers are hand-finished. Suspension front and rear is about as flash as it gets: mammoth 2in diameter inverted forks with TIN coated tubes. The rear monoshock has a remote preload adjuster to go with its shock-mounted rebound and compression adjusters, and the front end is multi-adjustable, too.

Believe it or not, this monster actually handles. Like the

Produced	2008-present
Engine Size	1679cc
Cylinders	4
¼ mile sprint	10.86 secs
Top Speed	143mph
Power Output	174.3bhp
Transmission	Manual
Gears	5 speed, slipper clutch, shaft drive
Seat Height	30.5in (775mm)
Weight	683lb (310kg)
Wheelbase	66.9in (1699mm)
(Specifications refer to the 2008 model)	

original VMAX (and to keep mass centralization as low as possible), the 15-liter fuel tank is mounted under the seat with the fuel filler positioned under the rider's backrest. Handlebars are posh, tapered items. An all-new instrument panel includes an analog tacho, digital speedo, plus LED shift lights. The info-center on the pseudo gas tank provides more information than you can imagine... throttle position, miles per gallon, and a stop watch just for starters. So let's go.

Yamaha YZF-R1

Manufactured by the Yamaha Motor Company since 1998, the Yamaha YZF-R1, or R1, is an open-class sport bike. Yamaha launched the YZF-R1 after completely redesigning the Genesis engine to offset the crankshaft, gearbox input, and output shafts. This compacting of the engine made the total engine length much shorter, significantly shortening the wheelbase, resulting in much quicker handling and an optimized center of gravity.

Superbike experts reckon this was the third and final great sports bike of the 1990s. The Honda Fireblade set the agenda, the Ducati 916 added finesse, and the Yamaha YZF-R1 topped them off with extra power and madness. Even today the original model is a sports tool to be reckoned with, and updated versions are even more potent and easier to use. The bike represents

Produced	1998-present
Engine Size	998cc
Cylinders	4
¼ mile sprint	10.19 secs
Top Speed	168mph
Power Output	150bhp
Transmission	Manual
Gears	6 speed, multi plate clutch
Seat Height	31in (800mm)
Weight	419lb (190.1kg)
Wheelbase	55.7in (1415mm)

(Specifications refer to the 1998 YZF-R1)

evolution at its finest – the technology's not hugely changed since the FZR1000 of 1989 but the YZF-R1 has always delivered a minimum of 150bhp (130 at the wheel). Torque is never in short supply and the bike's light weight makes the most of both.

The gearbox can be a little reluctant, but long-lasting problems with it are very rare. If you're thinking of buying, beware of race/track YZF-R1s that have been thrashed. Otherwise, there are no major problems and the finish is much better than early/mid-1990s Yamahas, but note the black finish on the frame and swingarm of 2003 models rubs off easily.

Reports claim this is a track bike to demolish rivals and wring the rider's adrenal glands dry: the original 1998-99 model was apparently the liveliest and hardest to tame. Later Yamaha YZF-R1s were easier to pilot, but don't think that means they're soft in any way. The original was slightly hard to turn into corners and could run wide: however, later versions were improved with a stiffer headstock and firmer forks. As you'd expect, there are ace brakes but, that apart, riders say with approval, extra equipment on a race rep just adds weight so features on the bike are pretty minimal.

Comfort's pretty good for a rider, although pillions must be brave. Headlights are effective even if the mirrors aren't brilliant. There's some underseat storage too – although on models from 2002, where exhausts occupy that space, it's minimal. On recent adapted YZF-R1s, Josh Hayes (US) has won the AMA Pro Superbike title three consecutive times from 2010-12, succeeded by compatriot Josh Herrin in 2013.

Yamaha YZF-R6

First introduced in 1998, the Yamaha YZF-R6 is a 600-class sport bike, significantly updated in 2001, 2003, 2006, 2008, and revised in the years in between and thereafter. This is a highly capable track bike that works supremely well on the road, too. When it first came out, it caught

the 600 race rep class napping and nothing came close until Suzuki launched its 2001 GSX-R600 – that's a long time to rule the 600 roost and shows just how good the original Yamaha YZF-R6 was.

So what's it like to ride? The engine really loves to rev – a 15500rpm redline was high for the time – and it's surprisingly powerful. A top speed of 160mph doesn't sound fantastically amazing in these days of 180mph bikes but unleashing the 108bhp certainly feels pretty special. The mid-range is surprisingly meaty, although the top-end rush hides it. The gearbox isn't the smoothest but aficionados claim it's at least a match for most rivals. Light, rapid steering makes it easy to handle and the bike is hard to fault on the track – ultimately, the pegs will touch down but that takes some doing. The bars will waggle under power but this is a fast-steering track bike so that's to

Produced	1998-present
Engine Size	599cc
Cylinders	4
¼ mile sprint	11.2 secs
Top Speed	160mph
Power Output	108bhp
Transmission	Manual
Gears clutch	6 speed, multi plate
Seat Height	32.8in (833mm)
Weight	399lb (181kg)
Wheelbase	54.4in (1382mm)

(Specifications refer to the 1998 model)

be expected. It can't quite match the composition and easy turn in of the latest supersport 600s but the difference is small – you'll find that chassis wear will be more significant on most machines.

The finish is a mixed bag. Plenty of major parts resist the rigors of rain and salt, but a few smaller parts let the superbike down. However, these minor niggles concerning the tendency of bolts, brackets, and fasteners plus a handful of bigger components to fur or rust up too easily, don't detract from the fact that major reliability problems are extremely rare. Prospective owners would do well to check for heavy oil consumption and any form of gearbox fault.

Despite what some say, sports bikes don't have to be crippling or impractical, and the YZF-R6 is neither. The riding position's pretty reasonable – touring is possible in comparative comfort, although the seat could benefit from a gel insert. Instruments are comprehensive for the era and include an extra trip meter triggered by the fuel reserve. Riders say that there is above average underseat storage, and that night/day visibility benefits from good headlights and passable mirrors.